The Invisible Disability And Me

by

Laura Lowles

Printed in the United Kingdom

First Printing, 2017

ISBN: 978-1-326-91696-1

PublishNation

www.publishnation.co.uk

Cover Design by Laura Lowles via Canva.com

Acknowledgements

A massive thank you to my husband, family and friends for your unwavering support through the difficult times and for refusing to give up. Without you, this journey would have been very different.

I would also like to offer my thanks to Hearing Link UK for their support, advice and guidance to not only me, but also to my family. Your work is invaluable for people who find themselves in the same position as I did and I hope that many, many more people will continue to be supported by your fantastic charity.

My thanks also go to all those who donated to my campaign on Kickstarter, this book would never have been published without your help. Special mentions go to the following individuals;

My wonderful mother Jacqueline Dillon, who not only supported me through my hearing loss journey, but also helped this book to become reality.

My lovely mother in law Rosemarie Clancy, who has been a great support to both me and my husband.

The beautiful Vicky Cooper, my maid of honour and the loveliest friend I could wish for.

And last but by no means least, a big thank you to the lovely Georgina Swift.

Your backing is very much appreciated, thank you!

A cheeky, surprise, special mention also goes to Jacqui Smith – Happy (belated) Christmas, Love from Alan.

Introduction

Laura Lowles is the writer of The Invisible Disability And Me blog and she has collaborated with Hearing Link UK, Restored Hearing, Hearing Wales and Everyday Hearing on guest blogs. She also wrote an article for the Autumn 2015 edition of the 'Living With Disability' magazine in partnership with Hearing Link as well as the July edition of Hearing Link's magazine "Hearing Matters". She has also been nominated for the Blogger Recognition Award and Sunshine Blogger Award by fellow bloggers.

Laura was born with significant hearing loss as a result of Maternal Rubella. She wore hearing aids from the age of two and attended mainstream primary and secondary school and went on to obtain a Law Degree at the University of Plymouth.

In 2014 whilst working as a Prosecutions Assistant, at the age of 27 she suffered with Sudden Sensorineural Hearing Loss and lost all the hearing in her right ear. Her life dramatically changed overnight and the hearing loss had a huge impact on her life.

Since then Laura has been trying to raise awareness of hearing loss and of the lesser known Sudden Sensorineural Hearing Loss amongst her peers and the wider community.

In December 2014, she received a Med-El Cochlear Implant from the Royal National Throat Nose and Ear in London. The device was activated in January 2015 and Laura immediately thrived. She continues to receive full advantage of her cochlear implant today.

In February 2016, she suffered a further bout of Sudden Sensorineural Hearing Loss and has subsequently lost what little hearing was left in her left ear. Fortunately, her implant continues to provide her with the hearing she needs, however, an adult without other sensory impairments are unable to receive two Cochlear implants under the NICE guidelines in the UK. This is something Laura passionately feels needs to be reviewed and changed.

Laura has written this book as a guide for those suffering with any degree of hearing loss or tinnitus as well as those going through the Cochlear Implant process. She hopes that through this book you will be able to pick up some useful tips and tricks to help you deal with the complexities of everyday life.

A word from the author Laura Lowles "I hope to be able to empower, educate and help those suffering from all forms of hearing loss, whether mild, severe or profound. My aim is to provide you with tips for coping with your hearing loss in any type of environement. It can be debilitating and exhausting I know, but with a few useful tricks you can make your life easier. Hearing loss, although always a huge part of your life, doesn't need to define who you are or prevent you from doing the things you love.

I hope that this book will help you feel more positive and hopeful about your future."

Contents

Finding out about the options available to you within the work environment and my helpful tips and advice on how to make your work environment a less daunting place.

Chapter Eight: Travel

Tips and Tricks for traveling with hearing loss or a cochlear implant.

Chapter Nine: Assistive Equipment

Exploring devices, equipment and apps that can help you on a day to day basis.

Chapter Ten: Cochlear implants

The what, why and how of cochlear implants and what to expect when you go through the CI process.

Chapter Eleven: Rehabilitation

Tips, advice and tools to help you get the most from your Cochlear Implant.

Chapter Twelve: My Journey Continues

My personal account of how my Cochlear Implant has affected my life.

End Note:

Note from the author.

Chapter One
My Journey

I have had hearing loss since birth; my mother contracted Rubella whilst pregnant and the virus attacked my ears and left scars behind my eyes. Despite this, I have never been considered Deaf. I grew up firmly in the hearing world and I was never treated any differently because of my hearing loss.

Despite having been born with a hearing loss, it took until I was 18 months old for a consultant to finally diagnose me with a moderately severe/severe sensorineural hearing loss and at the age of two I was fitted with bilateral hearing aids.

By all accounts I was a happy, cheeky and confident child and my hearing loss never adversely affected me. I had intensive speech therapy from a young age and was also taught to touch type whilst in primary school, which has served me well in my adult years working in offices. My parents were careful to ensure that my hearing loss was never used as an excuse for any bad behaviour nor was it used to give me any special treatment, I think they were possibly harder on me at times because they didn't want my hearing to be an excuse for my conduct.

I attended mainstream primary and then secondary school, making some wonderful friends who, 19 years later are still by my side. There were of course, some aspects of my early life that were different to my peers; I had many hospital appointments to keep an eye on my hearing levels, speech and language therapist visits at school and occasionally assistive equipment, which I always rejected. I was, and I remain, just 'Laura'.

From memory, I never experienced any negative attitudes to my hearing loss, for which I count myself lucky. Children were obviously naturally curious about my hearing aids but they were never nasty or mean about it and it often was forgotten instantly. I was a confident and happy child; my parents often remind me that I was that child that could be found hanging off a tree backwards taking no notice as to whether my hearing aids would survive my latest adventure.

As a teenager, my experience was slightly different. I was a lot more aware that I was different to my peers and I hated having my hearing aids on show. It didn't help that I also wore braces and glasses and felt like a 'geek'. I wore my hair down to detract attention from the aids and I became more concerned with how people would perceive them, especially the opposite sex.

I made the conscious decision at the age of about 13 or 14 to only aid my right ear as I felt I wasn't getting any benefit from wearing the left aid. This was fully supported by my parents and consultants and had little effect on my life. I didn't get an enormous benefit from wearing an aid in that ear so only minor adjustments were needed to compensate for the loss, such as walking on the left side of people so that speech could be heard in my right ear. A very tiny inconsequential change, but one that made a difference to me and stuck – now everyone knows which side to walk on.

There were more things, again minor, that I missed out on as a teenager but at that age they seemed life altering.

Taking part in 'Chinese Whispers' and sleepovers were a minefield. Whispers were impossible for me to hear and for a while this was combatted by myself and the person "whispering" stepping outside of the classroom and talking normally. This worked for a while but eventually I became too aware of being the odd one out and became self-conscious about whether I was whispering or shouting when it came to my turn as I couldn't gauge the tone of my voice effectively. In the end, I decided to decline to take part and I remember sitting on the side-lines feeling sorry for myself whilst everyone else was in fits of giggles.

Sleepovers, whilst fun and an integral part of any girl's childhood, were another obstacle for me. I was afraid of missing out on some important piece of gossip or a funny joke so only took my hearing aid out when I was completely sure that everyone was fast asleep. Waking up was even worse; I was and still am to an extent, a heavy sleeper and without my hearing aid in, I worried that everyone else would be wide awake and busy chatting away or eating breakfast downstairs whilst I was still deep in slumber hours later. It meant I either slept with my hearing aid in and risked the batteries dying or I took my hearing aid out and slept pitifully, waking often to check whether the others were still asleep.

Aside from these minor setbacks, I don't think anyone ever gave a second thought about my hearing loss or even knew I had a hearing aid when meeting me for the first time. I had, and still have, thanks to the earlier speech therapists, excellent verbal communication skills and interact "normally", whatever that means.

I remember one occasion whilst at University coming back from the Christmas break in our first year, I had my hair tied up after a 5-hour coach journey (and probably a hungover to boot), walking into our flat to hear one of our housemate's comment "oh look, Laura got a hearing aid over Christmas". I was shocked (and secretly delighted) that they hadn't cottoned on to it earlier and it boosted my confidence immeasurably, so much so that these days I am often found with my hair tied up at the top of my head, although that's probably because I am too lazy to style it any differently really.

Life plodded on in this way throughout my teens and early to mid-twenties; hearing levels staying stagnant and, with the exception of an upgrade to digital aids, (the audiologist remarked that my hearing aids belonged in a museum they were that old!) things remained the same. I had a Law degree, a good job, good friends, family, partner and social life. I was happy and enjoying my life.

I was never told that my hearing levels could change and they didn't change for 25 years. I never expected that they could change so dramatically, and so suddenly, which is what happened at the grand old age of 27.

A few days after my 27th birthday I woke up to muted hearing in my right ear and a feeling that I and everyone around me were underwater. It was a bizarre feeling and one I wasn't comfortable with. I booked a GP appointment for the following day where I was advised I had glue ear and sent home with decongestants. Over the next two days' things progressively got worse, I could barely hear on the telephone and had constant, roaring tinnitus which was blocking what little noise I could hear. I woke up three days after the onset of symptoms and could not hear a thing. I couldn't hear myself talking or even hear the door slamming. I was distraught. I burst into floods of tears, terrified that this could be permanent.

My partner immediately took me to the Accident & Emergency department of our local hospital where I was seen by a consultant who performed a short examination of my eardrum and diagnosed a perforated eardrum despite the lack of discharge and other associated symptoms. She, like the GP, sent me on my way with decongestants. Whilst myself and my partner were somewhat placated, there was still a niggling doubt in my mind and so my mother booked an appointment for a few days later with my ENT consultant.

It was at this appointment that I finally had an updated audiometry test which showed that I had suffered a sudden and dramatic decrease in my hearing levels propelling my hearing into the profound range. The consultant explained that this was permanent and irreversible, known as Sudden Sensorineural Hearing Loss. He advised us that the only medication that *could* make a difference were steroids, of which I was given a hyper-intensive course for 12 days. This treatment, he warned, was not always effective, especially after 72 hours of the onset of symptoms but at this point I was willing to try anything.

For those twelve days on steroids, I was in limbo. I was constantly wondering whether the treatment was working; ringing little bells and slamming doors every day to check whether I could detect any changes in hearing. It was a constant rollercoaster of emotions; one minute I would feel upbeat, channelling a 'Positive Mental Attitude' and telling myself that the steroids were working and the next, a downward spiral, feeling isolated, lonely and scared.

The steroid treatment had no impact on my hearing levels and this is when I began to realise that this is what my life would now be like, that I would for the rest of my life, struggle to communicate, to take part and to enjoy the little things in life. I was borderline depressed.

The ENT consultant broached the subject of Cochlear Implants and I shot him down straight away. I didn't know much about the device and the thought of having surgery for something that wasn't guaranteed scared me. I don't mind admitting that vanity also played a part in my rejection of an implant, I didn't want a clunky eyesore visible for everyone to see, clearly marking me out as different.

Once I had time to digest the diagnosis, I began to fully research Cochlear Implants. It took many, many weeks of Googling, emailing hearing charities and pondering before I decided it was worth pursuing. My consultant was contacted and a referral to a cochlear implant hospital 10 miles away was made.

In the meantime, I struggled to cope with everyday life. I went back to my GP and was signed off work for a month whilst I tried to come to terms with what this diagnosis meant and how it would affect my normal life.

I became a shadow of the former Laura; where I was once confident, outgoing and bubbly, I became withdrawn, shy and isolated. I withdrew from my family and friends and relied heavily on a handful of people, mainly my mother and my partner. At that point in time, I felt I had nothing to offer people, I couldn't take part in group conversations, I couldn't keep in contact with friends and family by telephone and I was generally not in a good frame of mind.

For the first time in my life I became scared of the outside world. I thought heavily about whether I would get injured or killed crossing the road and the more I thought about these scenarios, the more I didn't want to interact with life outside my four walls.

I also became obsessed with Googling 'Sudden Sensorineural Hearing Loss', trying to cling on to any piece of hope that I could find. I read somewhere that some people spontaneously get all or some their hearing back, sometimes weeks or months after the prognosis so I hoped that I would be one of the lucky ones. Unfortunately, I wasn't.

I also obsessed about the things that could happen around the home; my partner occasionally works night shifts and I worried that I wouldn't be able to hear the fire alarm or if someone was burgling our property. It caused many sleepless, anxiety riddled nights.

Not long after my diagnosis, my partner proposed to me and whilst it is, and was, a wonderful memory that I will never forget, there are parts of it that I feel I missed out on. I feel selfish saying it out loud but I will always remember the fact that I couldn't hear his exact words as he asked me to marry him – perhaps he never asked me to marry him at all and he was just showing me a pretty ring – too late now anyway!

As time went on, and the nearer it got to my return to work date, I decided to not dwell on the negatives too much and instead focus on the things I could do such as baking, reading and swimming. I filled my time with these activities and with a heavy heart, counted down the days until I returned to 'reality'.

The return to work was as scary as I imagined; from the crowded, busy bus full of screaming school children that I couldn't hear, to the hurried, tense crossing of roads and the reality of working in an open plan office. Don't get me wrong, my employers were wonderful and supportive, but no one can prepare you for the shock of realising you are ill equipped, mentally, physically and emotionally, to carry out your job and communicate with your colleagues.

There was so much of my job that I could no longer do; the most important of which was communication via telephone. As I work in an environment where sensitive, confidential matters are dealt with, much of our communication is by telephone. Large parts of my job were delegated to my manager and I was left essentially just inputting data all day – nothing wrong with that, but not what previously I did nor what I wanted to do.

Meetings were another integral part of my job that I was unable to fulfil; I could not hear in an environment where several people were talking at once as I was unable to gauge where or who the sound was coming from. At times, I was the only person left in the office whilst the rest of the company were in meetings, further fuelling my feelings of inadequacy and isolation.

The constant strain of having to concentrate so hard to listen to people, coupled with debilitating tinnitus, left me feeling exhausted by the end of the day and I suffered with migraines daily. You don't realise how much it takes out of you but it constantly left me feeling weak and run down. I felt at my lowest at this point, when it was abundantly clear that I couldn't cope.

A few weeks after the diagnosis, myself, my partner and a few friends headed off to Thailand on a pre-booked holiday. I had so looked forward to the holiday when we had spontaneously booked it a few months prior, to meet up with one of our friends on her three-month adventure around the world, but now I felt anxious.

Travel has always been something I have loved and now it felt like there were so many things that could go wrong; maybe I would miss the tannoy announcements at the airport and miss my flight, or not be able to hear the cabin crew giving their safety demonstrations if there was an accident on board, what would I do to entertain myself for 14 hours as I could not hear the inflight movies, and would I miss out on the buzz of Bangkok city and the excited chatter of my friends eagerly making plans for our two weeks in South east Asia?

Whilst I loved the holiday itself and spending two weeks relaxing with my friends, we had a full-on schedule; visiting 5 destinations in just 14 days - taking in the buzzing city of

Bangkok, the full moon party in Kho Phangnan, the backpacking haven of Ko Samui and the small fishing island of Kho Tao - it was a lot less relaxing than I thought. It is always tricky communicating whilst abroad even if you do not have a hearing loss, but having to rely on someone else to do the communicating for you can feel demeaning and I felt a little useless whenever something went wrong - like my partner's backpack going missing on route to the small islands. Whilst I tried to do my best to help locate the backpack all I felt I was really doing was adding to the panic. We did eventually get the backpack back; in case you were wondering.

No holiday to Thailand is complete without a trip to the legendary Full Moon Party and I had been so excited to experience this but I couldn't hear the music so the 'buzz' just wasn't there for me. That said, my partner and friends were amazing, they never made me feel like I was anything other than the person they have known for years and when I couldn't hear a song that knew I loved, they mouthed the words for me so I could hear it in my head – it was a reminder of how amazing these people are and continue to be.

Back in good old Blighty we had other things to plan and navigate our way through – our engagement party and wedding! We had planned on having a small get together with our families to celebrate our engagement once we were back but this escalated into a party with all our friends too. It was a wonderful night seeing everyone we loved in one place, celebrating our future but it was also the first time I had seen many of my family and friends since the hearing loss and I really struggled.

In hindsight, we probably shouldn't have chosen to hold the party in a section of a bar on a busy Saturday night; the noise from other customers and background music only served to make my situation even more prominent. I remember my dad talking to my boss and his wife and calling me over to ask me a question, I couldn't hear him at all. I had to ask him to repeat the question about three times and then ended up just laughing (something I regularly do when I haven't heard what is being said). My dad, my boss and his wife all looked to me for an answer to a question I hadn't heard, I felt so embarrassed. I knew it wouldn't matter to them, and that they understood but I felt so uncomfortable and self-conscious that I excused myself and went off to the ladies' room for a bit of a cry.

In some respects, I am lucky that I live in an era where technology is abundant and in certain situations it has made communication less stressful and a lot less complicated. Wedding planning was a prime example of this. I did all my research online and talked to our chosen suppliers via email – we did meet with the important suppliers face to face too but generally, it was all organised via the wonders of the world-wide web and what a life saver that was.

It was mid-June before I had any consultations about a Cochlear Implant, four months after the diagnosis. I had been warned beforehand that the process could be lengthy and tedious but nothing could have prepared me for how I would feel during the process.

The process itself involved a lot of consultations, hearing tests, speech perception tests, lip reading tests, CT and MRI scans. I knew my hearing levels were in the profound range but I hadn't quite comprehended how bad my speech perception levels were.

In a sound proof, deathly silent room, my overall speech perception levels were just 12% with both ears aided. 12%! With just my left ear aided the levels came down to 9% and my right ear scored a whopping 0%, in fact the test wasn't fully completed because it was obvious to the audiologist that I simply couldn't hear anything and that I was getting more and more agitated and emotional about it.

That 0% scared me. What scared me even more was that the hospital refused to accept me onto the Cochlear Implant programme because my hearing levels in my left ear were deemed slightly out of the NICE criteria acceptable range, by a whole 5 decibels. That's a whisper. I was refused an implant on the grounds of a freaking whisper.

Luckily, I had family and an ENT consultant who refused to give up and I was referred to another hospital 16 miles away and the process begun again.

A further speech perception test carried out at the new hospital three months after the first showed that my hearing in the left ear had deteriorated slightly and that I was now on the borderline for the NICE criteria. The audiologists were confident that this wouldn't be an issue and put me forward for an implant. From this point onwards, everything snowballed.

In November, a mere three weeks after the decision was made to give me an implant, I was invited back to the hospital to choose a device and talk through any issues I had with a small group of other prospective implantees. I felt hopeful walking into this meeting and was excited that I could have a choice in what implant I received as many people cannot due to underlying medical reasons. I had spent countless hours researching the three different manufacturers and the devices they had on offer and had made spreadsheets, flowcharts and drew up a list of questions to ask the audiologist. I wasn't going in ill prepared.

My personal choice was down to two devices by different manufacturers, I was leaning towards one device but it was purely on aesthetics. The thing with Cochlear Implants is that the results are all subjective. No one, including the audiologists, surgeons and speech therapists, knows how your brain is going to react and adapt to the implant so it is impossible to choose a device based on concrete evidence. Whilst I had researched the recall rates, and the different software available, there wasn't much difference between them to be perfectly honest. However, on the day of the choice, the audiologist informed us that one of the devices had to be withdrawn due to a recent recall of their latest batch due to moisture issues – the device in question was my second choice and it felt like this was a sign. A very good sign.

Two weeks after choosing my device, I received an email from the hospital whilst at work asking me if I was able to have my operation the following week. This freaked my mother out a bit as she wasn't prepared for it to happen so soon. I however thought "why wait". I knew I would have the operation at some point and the lead up to Christmas and New Year was the perfect period for me to take time off to recover and return in the New Year fresh and full of optimism.

I had a week to get all my work completed, tie up the loose ends, get my Christmas presents sorted and prepare myself for my first ever operation – scary stuff! Having so little time to get everything prepared and in order beforehand meant that I didn't have time to dwell on the situation, or more specifically, the dangers of the operation such as the increased risk of contracting meningitis, infection or simply the implant not providing any benefit and so I was relatively calm come operation day. I can't say the same for my family though.

The operation in itself was fairly "unremarkable" as my hospital notes state. The surgeon had declared it a total success and I was discharged a mere 10 hours after I arrived.

I couldn't have imagined just how much the implant would change my life and how much benefit I would get from it. I had deliberately kept my expectations low, as in medical terms, Cochlear Implants are still a new and emerging technology.

The implant not only brought me a sense of hearing back, it brought me back to life. For the 11 months I had lived without my hearing I had felt I was only living a part of my life.

Now the fun could begin.

Chapter Two
What Is Hearing Loss?

Hearing loss

Noun

1. "an increase in the threshold of audibility caused by age, infirmity, or prolonged exposure to intense noise" Collins English Dictionary

Hearing is one of the five human senses along with taste, touch, sight and smell but sometimes we do not recognise the value of this important sense until it is gone.

Hearing Loss is extremely common; there are an estimated 11 million[1] people in the UK of all ages living with some degree of hearing loss and this is estimated to rise to 15.6 million by 2035. More than 900,000 of these people suffer with severe or profound hearing loss.

Hearing loss from a medical point of view is the result of sound signals not reaching your brain and there are two main types of hearing loss;

Sensorineural Hearing Loss which is caused by damage to the fragile hair cells inside the inner ear or by damage to the auditory nerve. Some causes of sensorineural hearing loss include viral infections of the inner ear, Meniere's disease, meningitis or genetic abnormalities. This is the most common type of hearing loss.

---

[1] Action on Hearing Loss https://www.actiononhearingloss.org.uk/

Sensorineural hearing loss is permanent and irreversible.

Conductive Hearing Loss is when sounds are unable to pass from your outer ear to your inner ear, normally a result of a blockage. Common causes of conductive hearing loss are build-up of ear wax or fluid from an ear infection.

Conductive hearing loss is usually temporary and can be treated.

Recognising the type of hearing loss you have is the first step towards obtaining effective treatment, preventing further loss or improving what hearing you do have.

Losing your hearing can be so gradual that you barely notice or it can be sudden, overnight; regardless, losing your hearing in any way is a traumatic event. Early signs of hearing loss can be as subtle as having to slightly turn up the volume on the television or your telephone or even mishearing a few words here and there. Other symptoms can include hearing a ringing in your ears (tinnitus) or noticing the quality of your hearing is distorted or sounds are 'hollow'. If you experience any of these symptoms, seek the advice of an Audiologist or an Ear Nose Throat consultant as soon as possible.

Hearing loss can be a common result of aging and this is still regarded amongst the public as the number one cause of hearing loss. As you get older, the fragile structure of the inner ear begin to lose their functionality and break down, causing gradual hearing loss. However, exposing yourself to loud noises such as concerts, gun shots and heavy machinery in the workplace can also cause hearing loss to occur as loud noises damage the structure of your inner ear, this can cause hearing loss at a faster rate than the aging process. With the advancement of technology this could explain why we have seen a rise in younger people with hearing loss.

There are also instances where hearing loss cannot be explained.

Hearing loss

Noun

2. "a sensory loss that impacts on every aspect of daily life."
Laura Lowles

My own hearing loss was sudden, profound and devastating. There has been no definitive reason provided for why I suddenly lost my hearing again at 27 years of age. Various consultants have deliberated over the cause, numerous MRI and CAT scans have been carried out but the best reason I have been given for my hearing loss is a "viral infection", despite the fact that I was in fine health immediately before.

The hearing loss occurred over several days; I had noticed a muted sensation in my right ear (my "good ear" prior to the loss) and a feeling that I was speaking underwater. It was bizarre. I consulted my GP who diagnosed glue ear and was sent off on my way with nasal sprays and various other decongestants. My symptoms failed to improve, until one day approximately 4 days after the onset, I woke up to no hearing at all. I couldn't even hear myself speak. I was distraught.

A trip to my local Accident & Emergency centre revealed (wrongly) that I had a perforated eardrum. However, I was not happy with this diagnosis, especially as I had no pain or discharge and so I consulted my ENT surgeon the following day.

Pure tone audiometry test and bone conduction tests were carried out which discovered I had suffered a sudden and dramatic hearing loss. My hearing levels were now in the profound region and I was unlikely to get benefit from hearing aids.

For me, hearing loss was isolating. I felt very vulnerable and exposed and it took a long time to come to terms with it.

As with all medical situations, especially ones that are permanent and life changing, there are many emotions you may go through whilst dealing with your loss, below are just some of some of the emotions I went through and ones you might find you feel too.

Sadness

I remember feeling incredibly sad when I lost my hearing to SSHL, sadness for what I used to be able to do and sadness for what I felt I would never be able to achieve. You go through a stage of mourning for your old life and wishing that things could be as simple.

Confusion

After you start to get past the mourning, your thoughts may inevitably turn to why? Why did this happen? Why did it happen to me? What could I have done to prevent it? You may feel confused as to what brought on the hearing loss and unable to find the answers you want.

Frustration

A feeling of frustration comes with the confusion. You may feel frustrated because you can never get the answers as to why you lost your hearing, frustration because you cannot do anything to prevent further loss, and frustration for all the things you cannot do because of your reduced hearing.

Dependence

As you begin to get used to your hearing loss, you can find yourself becoming more dependent on key members of your family. For me, this was my mother and my husband. I depended on them being there to help me if I couldn't understand what people were saying, if I was going somewhere new I relied on them to help me navigate the way. It's a natural step but one that can be incredibly demeaning for a previously independent person.

Guilty

I felt incredibly guilty for a period of time; guilty because I was missing out on my family and friends lives because of my own feelings of inadequacy, guilty because I was relying on certain family members to help me with my day to day life and guilty because I couldn't do my job as well as I wanted to.

Helplessness

Without being able to hear what is going on around you, you can end up feeling helpless in certain situations, especially when you are by yourself. Things like crossing the road or communication with complete strangers are all things that make you feel scared and alone. I felt incredibly useless at work, so much of my role I was unable to fulfil because I couldn't hear on the telephone etc.

Denial

I think everyone goes through this with any medical situation. You try to kid yourself that everything is normal, that you can do everything you used to do and that this is just a temporary blip. Unfortunately for many, this isn't the case.

Defiance

Like denial, you become more determined to do things for yourself and to get your old life back. Out of rebelliousness you try to struggle your way through things by yourself.

Desperation

Once you begin to realise you cannot do all the things you want to, you become desperate. Desperate to find a cure, desperate to find information, anything! For me this came when I was prescribed oral steroids and was told they *might* work. I was desperate for them to work and adopted a "Positive Mental Attitude", telling myself daily that the steroids *were* working, that they *would* work etc. I also prayed to God to help me every day and researched the condition until my brain hurt.

Acceptance

Eventually you will begin to accept your condition, your new life and you will find ways to adapt that suit you. It doesn't need to change who you are as a person; you will just need to adapt to it so it doesn't consume your everyday life.

The important thing to remember is that in time things *will* get better!

Chapter Three

How To Cope With Hearing Loss

Understanding hearing loss and dealing with it are two completely separate things; you may know everything there is to know about hearing loss but be unable to cope with it in your everyday life. It is something that can impact on every part of your life from social situations to the work environment and everything in between.

This chapter aims to give you examples and practical advice on how to deal with your hearing loss. Remember, hearing loss is very much a personal condition and there unfortunately is no one size fits all approach.

Below are a few scenarios that you might face whilst dealing with hearing loss and some advice on how to handle the situation so that you can feel more included socially and professionally.

Scenario One: You are meeting your friends at a local, busy pub and are worried about whether you will be able to hear them.

Advice/Tips: There are several things you could do in this situation;

- *Ask your friends if you can move locations, choose somewhere where there is less of a crowd, maybe somewhere you are already familiar and comfortable with.*

- *If you are able to change the location, think about factors such as lighting and flooring that can have an effect on background noise – i.e. choose somewhere with carpet rather than wooden floors so the noise of chairs scraping and heels clicking won't disturb you.*

- *If changing the location isn't an option, think about where you can sit to minimise the background noise and maximise the impact of the person speaking to you; i.e. choose to sit with your back to the wall so that you will not be too disturbed by the background noise and facing the person/people you are with so you can read their lips.*

- *Similarly, try to choose a table where there is ample lighting. Bad lighting can make it very difficult to lip-read.*

- *If the venue is loud because of music, ask the staff if they could lower it and explain that you have a hearing loss and find it difficult to hear people over excessive noise. They should, in theory, be accommodating to your request.*

- *If you have one, bring a personal loop system with you. This works better when there is a small group – place the microphone in front of the person speaking or the middle of the table, in theory, the loop system should cut out the background noise for you.*

Scenario Two: You are required to attend a big meeting at work.

Advice/Tips: Meetings and large groups are always incredibly difficult to navigate, however, there is equipment you can utilise and things you can do to in this scenario;

- *Ask the organiser whether you can have the PowerPoint presentation (if applicable) or agenda in advance of the meeting, this way you can familiarise yourself with the topics that will be discussed.*

- *Sit yourself at the forefront of the meeting so that you are facing all the other delegates, this way you will at least be able to pinpoint who is speaking and attempt to lipread.*

- *Again, a personal loop system might be advantageous to you in this situation, especially if there are aren't too many people taking part/speaking.*

- *Consider requesting a 'Remote Speech To Text Reporter', this works in that the reporter is added to the meeting via a Skype connection and they translate all speech spoken to text which you will be able to follow.*

Scenario Three: You need to contact someone by telephone but struggle to hear clearly.

Advice/Tips: This is something that affects those with hearing loss a lot, it even happens to those with "normal" hearing too! Here are a few tips you can try out;

- *Try to use a mobile phone over an analogue phone, the connection is clearer and has a lot less interference.*

- *Switch your hearing aid/Cochlear Implant to the 'T' coil, this will cut out background noise and provide a clearer connection.*

- *If you wear a Cochlear Implant, consider using an accessory cable connected directly to your mobile phone and cochlear implant, this will mean that you won't have to struggle finding the right position for your CI microphone and will also mean that no one else can hear your conversation.*

- *If you are struggling to hear on the telephone, consider using the Text Relay service NGT (mobile phones) or a speech to text analogue phone.*

Scenario Four: You cannot hear the doorbell or fire alarm in your house.

Advice/Tips: This is something all hard of hearing people struggle with and is the cause of much anxiety. Do not panic! There are things you can do to make you feel safe and secure in your home.

- *Obtain a Bellman Paging 868 System which connects to your doorbell, fire alarm, baby monitor and telephone. It contains a vibrating mat which you can place under your pillow whilst asleep and a control pad which you can clip onto a piece of clothing whilst you are around the house. The control pad lights up a picture matching the corresponding sound alert.*

- *Consider obtaining a security camera which you can remotely control from your mobile phone or computer, it will also alert you to any detected activity in the zone set (i.e. directly outside your front door).*

- *Sign up to the 999-text service so that in an emergency you can contact the police, ambulance or fire service via text message (more information further on in this chapter).*

- *For those living alone, consider a hearing dog. The dog can alert you to the sound of an alarm or doorbell and can also be a companion too.*

- *If you live in a block of flats or a close neighbourhood, make your neighbours aware of your hearing loss so that in the case of emergency they can make sure you are safe or alert the emergency services to your hearing loss.*

We also have tips if you are looking to communicate with someone who is hard of hearing or vice versa detailed below. Remember, communication is a two-way street and you must be prepared to make some compromises along the way.

Top Communication Tips

For the hearing

- Face the person you are talking to directly so that they can read your lips if necessary.

- If you are not facing the person or they are not aware of you speaking, try to draw their attention to you, this can be by tapping them on the shoulder for example.

- Do **NOT** over exaggerate your facial expressions or words as this can make things harder if attempting to read lips.

- Try to sit in a well-lit position as dark environments will make it a lot harder to lip read.

- If possible, try to avoid overly noisy environments, especially if you are in a large group as it will be hard to concentrate on all the different sounds.

- Try to resist the urge to shout, as mentioned before volume is often not the issue in these circumstances.

- Speak clearly, at a moderate pace. Too quickly and the hearing-impaired individual may not be able to catch what you are saying, too slow there is a tendency to over exaggerate mouth movement which makes lip-reading harder.

- Do **NOT** hide your mouth as not only will sound be muffled, but it will make lip-reading impossible.

- If you are suddenly changing the direction of a conversation, perhaps let the hearing-impaired individual know by saying one word that is relevant to the new conversation so that they are aware they need to adjust their train of thought.

- A really important tip is to remember to speak to the hearing-impaired person, not to another person. I cannot remember how many times I have been passed over conversation simply because the person speaking did not know how to help me understand them.

Top Communication Tips

For the hearing impaired

- Maintain a sense of humour; yes, you will get words wrong sometimes but it can be a way of bringing you closer to the speaker rather than making you feel embarrassed – especially if the misheard word is a rude one!

- Tell people what works for you – no one knows better than you how you pick up conversation.

- Anticipate and try to combat difficult environments – for example, if you are meeting friends for dinner, ask if you can choose the location – sit with your back to a wall rather than to a crowded restaurant as this will reduce the amount of noise coming from different directions – some people find places with carpets easier etc.

- Pay attention – I know this will sound trivial and obvious but you will need to concentrate a lot harder on conversations than those with normal hearing.

- Look for visual clues to help you.

- Try not to interrupt the speaker mid flow as you may find as the conversation progresses you can fill in the gaps yourself with what additional information you were able to pick up.

- On the other hand, if you are really struggling, then do not be afraid to interrupt and ask the speaker to repeat themselves.

- Carry a pen and paper, if you are unable to follow a conversation, possibly ask if they could write it down.

Of course, not all communication goes smoothly and there are bound to be fails along the way – I know I've had many! Lip-reading is full of opportunities for misinterpreting people and is actually a lot harder than people give credit for. It takes a lot of concentration and in reality, is less than 30% accurate so no wonder we can get it wrong at times.

I always thought I was excellent at lip-reading but relying on it every day only highlighted how much you can get wrong, no matter how good you think you are. Music lyrics is one that I have struggled and still to this day struggle with, I often just make up the lyrics to suit me, which can lead to some embarrassment when you start singing the song out loud!

Even simple sentences can be misconstrued when you are lipreading, think about the following sentences/words and how they look when you say them – not so easy now is it!

What Was Said: I Love You

What I Thought: *Olive Juice / Elephant Shoes / Island View*

What Was Said: You're an Idiot:

What I Thought: *You're hideous*

What Was Said: Show Me

What I Thought: *Stupid*

What Was Said: Do you want a crème caramel?

What I thought: *Do you want curry powder?*

Whilst this might provide a few laughs along the way, it might also make you feel embarrassed, alone and isolated in dealing with your hearing loss. Please do remember that there are a myriad of resources, organisations and charities that can and will offer you advice, help and support along the way. It is important to reach out and ask for their help, so you can regain your independence and feel like a functioning member of society, which is something that I struggled with.

Charities and Organisations;

Hearing loss charities are an excellent source of advice and support, many individuals behind the charities have first-hand experience of dealing with hearing loss themselves or through a family member and can offer valuable support, especially if you are living alone.

Below is a (non-exhaustive) list of organisations and charities that I have either personally used, or I feel can offer support to those of you suffering from hearing loss, some of these have been mentioned previously.

Hearing Link UK;

Hearing Link are a registered UK charity set up to assist those with hearing loss, of all varieties. They assist people through their helpdesk, answering emails, putting people in touch with others in similar positions and offering courses. One such course is their Intensive Rehabilitation Programme which is a week-long course (free to yourself) designed to help you cope with your hearing loss in a practical way and in an environment where you feel safe, with people of all ages in similar positions to yourself.

To find out more about Hearing Link UK, have a look at their website; www.hearinglink.org

Action on Hearing Loss;

Another UK registered charity, formerly known as the RNID, their aim is to help those with hearing loss, tinnitus, cochlear implants and other hearing related conditions. Their website provides a wealth of information as well as videos and statements not only from people they have helped but also videos showing the extent and impact of hearing loss, to raise a more general awareness of it can affect lives.

You can also buy specialist equipment through their website, to find out more about Action on Hearing Loss have a look at their website www.actiononhearingloss.org.uk

Restored Hearing;

A Dublin based organisation designed to help you cope with Tinnitus. They are a start-up company with big aspirations to help prevent Tinnitus from occurring with lots of helpful advice on how to protect your hearing from excessive noise. They also have pioneered a "responsive sound absorbing technology which uses smart materials to absorb sound proportionally to the noise environment" called Sound Bounce which is an exciting development. They also developed a sound therapy, Sound Relief which is scientifically proven to alleviate the severity of tinnitus and currently offer a free 7-day trial of this for new customers.

You can find out more about their products here; www.restoredhearing.com

Your Local Council;

There are two ways in which the Council can offer you help, through their Adult Social Services Department who can help you with assistive equipment for your home. They will (usually) arrange a home visit to assess your needs and make a recommendation for you. Equipment such as the Bellman Paging System is available through the council and this system is designed to alert deaf or hard of hearing individuals to the doorbell, phone, baby monitor or fire alarm even when asleep.

Find your local council details here; https://www.gov.uk/find-local-council

Your local council could also offer some financial help through their disabled person's freedom pass scheme; if you have a severe/profound hearing loss and you live in a London borough, you may be eligible to apply for a Disabled Persons Freedom Pass which will entitle you to some free transport in your area or possibly UK wide.

Find out more about the 'Disabled Persons Freedom Pass' here; http://www.londoncouncils.gov.uk/services/freedon-pass/disabled-persons-freedom-pass

Hearing Dogs;

Hearing Dogs provide specially trained dogs for the hearing impaired. The dogs are trained to alert you to any noises, such as the doorbell, fire alarm etc and can prove invaluable to those living alone or with severe hearing loss. The waiting list is quite long because it can take several months to properly train a dog to the level required, however, it is always worth registering your interest, especially If you have a hearing loss that will further deteriorate over time.

You can register your interest in a Hearing Dog on their website www.hearingdogs.org.uk

British Cochlear Implant Group;

The BCIG is a professional organisation that represents all the cochlear implant centres throughout the UK. They offer comprehensive information on the ins and outs of cochlear implants and also have a very useful frequently asked questions section.

If you want to find out more about the BCIG, you can find them at www.bcig.org.uk

The Ear Foundation;

The Ear Foundation bridges the gap between the cochlear implant clinics and the local community where they are used such as schools and home and work environments. They offer services such as family programmes, an education programme and also offer a 'Sound Advice' programme designed to make the most of the new and emerging technology available.

Visit www.earfoundation.org.uk to find out more.

Connevans;

Connevans is an online (and physical) catalogue offering a wide range of products and equipment for the deaf or hard of hearing. They have products available for both personal and commercial consumers and have just about everything you could ever need. Their staff are also well equipped to answer any queries or concerns you may have about suitable devices. Their delivery service, I can personally say, is excellent.

To find out more about what products they offer have a look at www.connevans.co.uk

Access To Work;

More information on this is available in Chapter Seven.

999 Text Relay;

A vital service that lets deaf and hard of hearing people in the UK send a text message to the 999 emergency services where it will be passed on to the appropriate department. You do need to register your phone before using the service but is something that every deaf or hard of hearing person should do, even if just for peace of mind.

To register your phone visit www.emergencysms.org.uk

Chapter Four

Impact Of Hearing Loss And How We Can Help

Whilst we have talked about how hearing loss can make you feel, we haven't really discussed the impact that hearing loss can have on all aspects of your life, socially, mentally and professionally.

Socially

Helen Kellher once said "Blindness separates people from things; deafness separates people from people" and I completely agree. Although I don't know what it is like to be blind, I know what it is like to feel separate from my family, friends and peers and know how much sadness that feeling can bring.

Often people feel left out, as if they are personally being targeted as different when in fact it's simply because others do not know how to deal with their hearing loss or how to communicate with them and find it easier to overlook their needs entirely.

Those with smaller families or social groups are possibly more likely to be able to join in on conversations and events to a certain extent given the smaller number of people involved although it will of course, still be hard work and incredibly daunting.

It is much harder if you have a wide group of friends or a large, extended family as it is incredibly difficult to concentrate on speech in larger groups. Big events such as birthday parties, weddings and other celebrations are likely to be avoided for this very reason. Background noise is hard to cope with even in quiet environments so music and excessive chatter likely to be heard at these kinds of events would make even the most outgoing hearing impaired person want to shrivel up into a corner.

Constantly having to ask people to repeat their conversations, mishearing people or simply nodding along takes its toll on your self-confidence and you would be forgiven for wanting to escape the sympathetic looks as you ask someone to repeat their sentence for the fifth time but avoiding these situations not only affects your relationships but it also makes people less inclined to try to understand and assist you because they feel like you don't want to be a part of their lives. Catch 22 situation really.

Mentally

Those who suffer from some form of hearing loss are more likely to suffer with some form of mental illness, especially if they are isolated from their community and family. They are less likely to see a GP about any complaints because of communication issues which can lead to serious consequences.

Depression can be a grave consequence of hearing loss as a result of the isolation felt by the hearing impaired. Some feel as if they cannot carry on a social life because they are unable to communicate effectively and join in with conversations. Having some form of social life, whether extremely busy or sporadic makes individuals feel included in friendships and society as a whole.

A sense of belonging is vital to everyone's well-being. When you take away that ability you take away someone's self-worth and confidence. If you lose your confidence and begin to question your contribution to society you start to withdraw from everything and everyone and this further impacts upon your relationships with your family and friends creating a vicious circle that is hard to escape.

For some, underlying medical conditions that they are not aware of can be the contributing factor of their hearing loss. It is vital that if you do suffer from any form of hearing loss, you seek the advice of a medical expert so that other health conditions can be ruled out. Tinnitus is one such condition that could have an underlying medical reason for occurring and it can greatly impact upon your mental health with many people feeling as if they are going mad hearing sounds that no one else can.

Often those suffering from tinnitus find that they are extremely sleep deprived as they are unable to switch off those sounds, this coupled with the sheer amount of concentration it takes to focus on speech in everyday situations means that exhaustion is inevitable. With exhaustion, can come volatile mood swings and this can exacerbate depression and anxiety.

Professionally

We often portray a different persona in the workplace; more confident, self-assured and dominant than we are with our family and close friends. We take pride in the jobs and careers we have often worked or studied for years to obtain, and build up close friendships with our colleagues.

Those of us with a hearing impairment often struggle with this. How can we appear to others to be confident and expect them to take notice of us if we are struggling to hear and fulfil our jobs to the best that we can?

I was unprepared for how I would feel about returning to work following my hearing loss and it deeply affected me. I felt at my lowest whilst I was surrounded by the buzz of the office and not being able to participate in meetings and general office chatter.

So many jobs these days rely on telephone communication which is often a challenge for the hearing impaired, whilst there is equipment out there that can help on this front, I know I didn't want to have my shortfalls obvious to all and so I tried to carry on the best I could without the equipment. I eventually did have to consider specialist equipment but when it arrived it was unsuitable for our needs which of course, left me feeling even worse.

At the time, I felt that I had nothing to offer the company and felt that I was a hindrance to the rest of the office, whilst my colleagues were all wonderful to me, this is a feeling that stayed with me throughout. A lot of jobs out there are not suitable for the hearing impaired such as customer service and telesales and this can mean we are in jobs that we have no real passion for and can leave us feeling disenfranchised and lacking in motivation, neither of which are conducive to a content frame of mind.

How can we help?

More awareness needs to be made about the emotional effects of hearing loss and how we can help combat this.

Simple measures such as asking the hearing-impaired individual what we can do to help them converse more effectively would go a long way. It would prove that you are taking their feelings into consideration.

Teaching children skills to communicate with the hearing impaired and also lip-reading from a young age would not only prove worthwhile should they come into contact with someone with a hearing impairment or suffer with it themselves, but it could also improve their own cognitive learning. Similarly, schools should also be teaching children how to protect their hearing; prevention is the best cure.

Making companies deaf aware should also be a priority; with an estimated 11 million people in the UK suffering from some degree of hearing loss, there is likely to be some form of contact with a hearing-impaired person, whether it's an employee, client or customer. Being deaf aware would mean that they are able to treat the employee/client/customer according to their own individual needs and would save the embarrassment of miscommunication on either side and even potential loss of revenue.

Charities such as Action on Hearing loss run Deaf Awareness and Sign Language training for companies which aim to improve staff confidence and communication skills. They tailor their courses to meet the specific requirements of your company and are run by trainers who are deaf themselves, bringing a personal perspective to the course. It can even improve staff relations even if there are no hearing-impaired staff as the courses focus on communication as a whole.

Chapter Five

What is Sudden Sensorineural Hearing Loss?

What is it?

Sudden Sensorineural Hearing Loss (SSHL) commonly referred to as Sudden Deafness, it occurs when the inner ear or the nerve pathway between the ear and the brain becomes damaged, often for reasons unknown. It is described as an unexplained and rapid loss of hearing which usually occurs in one ear but sometimes in both. It can happen over the course of several days or rapidly all at once and is classed as a medical emergency.

It is typically diagnosed after a pure tone audiogram, or a hearing test to you and me, has been carried out. This will establish whether a loss has occurred, how much of a loss and in what frequencies. For SSHL to be diagnosed, there needs to be a loss of at least 30 decibels in three connected frequencies, to put that in perspective, a loss of this volume would make conversational speech sound more like a whisper.

To give you a further idea of hearing loss at different decibels, have a look at these common sounds;

Normal Conversation – 60-65dB

A Busy Street – 75-85 dB

Lawn Mower / Heavy Traffic – 85dB

Hand Drill – 98dB

Motorbikes – 100dB

Disco/Bar/Car Horn – 110dB

MP3 player on loud – 112dB

Chainsaw – 115-120dB

Rock Concert / Ambulance – 120DB

The below diagram shows what it looks like on an audiogram, note the difference between the "normal" hearing ranges and the profound range. Look at where the above examples would sit on the audiogram, you will begin to realise just how little hearing is left.

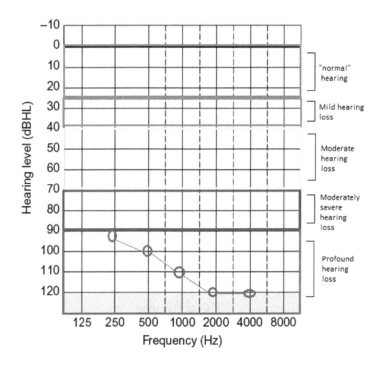

Whilst SSHL is not widely known amongst the public, it is estimated that over 150,000 people in the UK alone have suffered from sudden deafness[2]. It is not discriminate, and can occur at any age and in any sex so it is imperative that you know and look out for the early signs and seek treatment as soon as you can.

Treatment

Treatment for SSHL isn't widely known; in most cases steroids are prescribed either orally, and in high volume for a week or injected directly into the ear on three separate occasions. However, the benefit of these steroids is not completely identified. Specialists do say that steroids should be administered within 24-48 hours of the onset of symptoms for the best chance of regaining some or all of the lost hearing. The common consensus is that if the treatment is delayed by 72 or more hours, it is likely to be rendered useless.

It is believed that half of people diagnosed with SSHL will spontaneously recover some, if not all, of their hearing within 1-2 weeks of the onset of symptoms. However, this is not the case for all and should not be the cause of delaying any treatment.

What causes SSHL?

It is estimated that only 15%[3] of people that have been diagnosed with SSHL have an identifiable cause for their hearing loss which can include, but is not limited to, the following causes;

Infectious disease

Head trauma

---

[2] https://www.hearinglink.org/your-hearing/sudden-deafness-hearing-loss/what-is-sudden-deafness-hearing-loss/
[3] https://www.nidcd.nih.gov/health/sudden-deafness

Autoimmune diseases

Blood circulation problems

A tumour on the nerve that connects the ear to the brain

Disorders of the ear such as Meniere's Disease.

Whilst SSHL can be diagnosed from pure tone audiogram tests, it cannot be 100% verified as the ear is far too small to be examined in greater detail and no scans can give enough detail to determine the causes.

Most people who are diagnosed with SSHL have no known cause and it is often attributed to a "viral infection". This can be distressing because you do not know if it can occur again or if there are any preventative measures you can take to ensure that there isn't a repeat.

In fact, SSHL can (and in some cases, will) strike again which could leave you with a profound hearing loss in one or both of your ears. If there is no known cause of your SSHL, there is no telling when it could strike again.

What are the Symptoms?

Typical symptoms of SSHL include;

A loud 'pop' in the affected ear (a similar feeling to when you get off a plane)

Dizziness

Sensation of being underwater

Muted or distorted hearing

Ringing in the ear

Trouble understanding speech

Experiencing sounds that feel too loud and cause you pain

Feeling disconnected from your environment

An empty feeling in the affected ear

What should I do if I have these symptoms?

If you experience one, several or all of these symptoms, seek medical advice **IMMEDIATELY**. It is a medical emergency and you must treat it like so.

Seek the advice of a trained Ear Nose Throat Specialist or Audiologist where possible. You may find that your General Practitioner is unaware of SSHL (all the doctors I saw were unaware of it) and so you should prepare for your appointment by printing off information on SSHL, your nearest hospital with audiology facilities or hearing clinic for referral. Don't be afraid to push the point with them – it is your hearing that is at stake.

If they are unsure of what to do, ask for a Pure Tone Audiogram to be performed, this should at least alert them to who they need to refer you to. Make sure you also mention you need treatment within 24-48 hours so they are fully aware that this is urgent.

What can I do to prevent SSHL?

Whilst there is nothing definitive you can do to avoid SSHL (especially where causes are unknown) you can prevent general hearing loss by being pro-active and protecting your ears. Below are a few simple measures you can take to help protect your hearing;

Wear earplugs in extremely noisy environments (i.e. music gigs/work sites etc)

If you listen to music on a daily basis, turn down the volume. A good guide to whether your volume is too loud is whether you can hear background noise, if you cannot, it is too loud.

Turn down the volume on household devices such as the TV and radio. Small reductions can make a big difference.

Wear ear protectors when using noisy equipment (such as power drills and lawn mowers)

Keep an eye on your hearing levels; have routine testing for your hearing so you can track any differences.

Chapter Six

What is Tinnitus And How To Cope With It?

Tinnitus /' tɪnɪtəs'/

Noun

1. "a ringing, hissing or booming sensation in one of both ears..." Collins English Dictionary

2. "Although it is often referred to as "ringing in the ears", tinnitus can be perceived as many different sounds including hissing, clicking or whistling..." Medical News Today

What is tinnitus?

Tinnitus is commonly described as a ringing or buzzing in one or both ears that is only heard by the sufferer. It can vary in pitch, frequency and volume and can be very debilitating. It is said that we all suffer from very mild tinnitus, seemingly unaware of it until a trauma or a loss of hearing occurs. Some people will never be aware of their tinnitus and it is believed that some of us are just predisposed to the condition therefore more likely to suffer greatly from it.

It is thought that tinnitus occurs because of a problem with how the ear hears sounds and how our brains reacts and interprets them. Whilst the most common cause of tinnitus is hearing loss in some cases however, there appears to be no obvious problems with the ears or hearing. The only factor that the experts can agree on is that with most cases of tinnitus there appears to be no external source to the noise.

Whilst the general consensus is that tinnitus is a ringing or buzzing sound, the sounds can actually vary considerably from person to person. Tinnitus is a subjective condition and there are several different types of tinnitus such as 'pulsatile tinnitus' or 'vascular tinnitus' where people hear noises that beat in time with their pulse; this can sometimes be attributed to disturbances in the blood flow or other underlying medical conditions.

Causes

Tinnitus can develop gradually over time as our hearing deteriorates with age and the sounds become more prominent in our ears, it can also occur suddenly with no warning and this is normally linked to some form of hearing loss, such as Sudden Sensorineural Hearing Loss. Tinnitus is also thought to be linked to the following causes;

Inner ear damage

Middle ear infection

Menieres Disease

Perforated eardrum

Glue ear

Ear or head trauma

High blood pressure

High levels of stress

Exposure to loud sounds

Side effect of medication

According to the NHS, tinnitus is believed to affect around six million people or 10% of the UK population[4] to some degree with an estimated 600,000 people experiencing it severely with it impacting upon their day to day life in a significant way.

Treatment

Unfortunately, there is no miracle pill you can take to make tinnitus go away and most of us will suffer with the condition for the rest of our lives, but we will be able to manage it so that it is at a level that does not cause us distress. There is no one size fits all approach and you will need to experiment with different techniques to find what works for you.

Some of the most common "treatments" for tinnitus include

Music or sound therapy

Many people report that listening to music on a low volume helps to block out their tinnitus, perhaps this is because your brain is concentrating on alternative sounds.

Cognitive Behavioural Therapy

This is designed to try and examine your thought patterns and how you react. The idea is to retrain yourself to react in a different way, to not give your attention to the tinnitus and how it makes you feel.

Relaxation techniques

This is generally thought to be widely used for stress induced tinnitus with the idea being that the more relaxed you are, the less you will notice your tinnitus.

---

[4] http://www.nhs.uk/conditions/tinnitus/Pages/Introduction.aspx

Acupuncture

It is said, though not widely known, that acupuncture can help relieve tinnitus by altering the brains chemistry by reducing serotonin levels and also reducing inflammation.

Hearing aids or cochlear implants

In the case of severe hearing loss, hearing aids or cochlear implants can offer relief from tinnitus if it is connected to the loss of hearing.

My tinnitus occurred in my right ear when I lost my hearing and it was constant, loud and annoying. There was no one prevalent noise, instead it chose to manifest in a myriad of noises such as motorbikes, church bells, cats screaming and noises that to this day I cannot recognise. The consultants believed that the tinnitus was my brains way of trying to compensate for the loss of hearing, that it could no longer distinguish what noises were relevant or useless.

As the noises were constant I had trouble sleeping which exacerbated the tinnitus further until I was so stressed out about it that I suffered with migraines daily and slept sporadically. It was a vicious circle and one that appeared to be hard to break.

I received cognitive behavioural therapy during part of my cochlear implant process but it did little to alleviate the symptoms for me. Music was a no go as I had a profound hearing loss and struggled to hear anything that wasn't a pneumatic drill.

The thing that you don't get told about tinnitus is that it is *exhausting*. It is present from the moment you wake up to the moment you (try to) go to sleep. It can get in the way of your natural hearing and often make you feel like you are going mad as you never truly hear silence again. It can also make you feel so far removed from your environment; you know what sounds you should be hearing and you can see what is occurring around you but all you can hear is the tinnitus in your ears in whatever form it takes.

Along with sleep deprivation, tinnitus can result in mood swings, headaches and even in severe cases, depression.

I found that once I had received my implant the tinnitus became less of an issue, it is still there but it is much quieter and more manageable. I'm told this is because my brain has other noises to concentrate on and the tinnitus has been pushed to the background.

After my second bout of SSHL in my left ear, I found that I had tinnitus in both ears, although they were different sounds in each. As I only have a right sided implant it meant I was back to square one with constant noises in one ear. I was overjoyed – not.

As I've mentioned, there are techniques you can utilise and it is believed that over time, you will just get used to the sounds and learn to block them out. Though for the 600,000 odd of us that suffer with severe tinnitus it can be hard to do this.

Over time I have adapted to my tinnitus and come up with my own coping mechanisms – for example If I am struggling to get to sleep because of the noises, I make up stories in my head based on the sounds I can hear and lull myself to sleep. It often means I have some pretty crazy dreams but it seems to work for me!

Chapter Seven
Hearing Loss In The Workplace

I remember the day I came back to work after my hearing loss vividly. I was terrified. I hadn't ventured outside without support much in six weeks and here I was preparing to not only use public transport alone, but also spend 8 hours a day, 40 hours a week, in a large open plan office where I would essentially be less than useless.

I am lucky in that my commute to work is short (if the bus drivers and traffic permit of course) and the journey into work was over relatively quickly but it left an impact on my already frazzled state of mind. It was overwhelming, it was like an explosion of colours before my eyes and was disorientating. I could see all this action taking place but could not hear a thing. I felt like I was in a bubble and not entirely of my body.

Even now, there are parts of working in an open plan office that I hate. Even though I have an implant, I still have a hearing loss and still need to be aware of my surroundings and a lot of workplace environments are not conducive to those with hearing loss.

Here are my bug bears about coping with hearing loss at work;

- **Taking part in large meetings**; if meetings tend to get a little rowdy, it can be impossible to tell who is speaking or what they are saying and it can be a very stressful experience.

- **When multiple phones are ringing;** I have trouble distinguishing different phone tones and this means I often leave it too late to answer my phone as I am not aware that it is my extension ringing. On that note...

- **Talking to new people on the telephone**; generally speaking, I am perfectly fine with speaking on the telephone, especially with people I already know but there can be those occasions where someone you have never spoken to calls and you really struggle to hear them, this is made worse if they have any kind of accent or twang to their voice.

- **When people expect you to instantly recognise their voice**; another telephone related bug – it really irritates me when I answer my work extension and people just say "hello!" and instantly expect me to recognise their voice. It sometimes takes me a while to put a voice to a name on the phone and so I'm often winging it until I can recognise who it is.

- **When people approach you from behind and scare you**; my current desk unfortunately means my back is to the majority of the office and there have been several occasions when a colleague has come to talk to me and I have been completely unaware of them until they tap me on the shoulder and scare the life out of me!

- **When the office is loud**; obviously, this is something that happens to everyone and offices generally become noisy, especially at certain parts of the day but this makes listening to anyone quite difficult and exhausting.

- **When the office is too quiet;** I'm sounding a bit like Goldilocks here but when the office is too quiet it can make my tinnitus appear much, much louder which is just as irritating as a noisy office. Somewhere in the middle would be great!

- **Being introduced to new people**; There have been several occasions where I have been introduced to new starters and have completely misheard their names but have not realised until many, many weeks/months later.

- **When people use excessive jargon**; When you struggle on a daily basis to follow conversations, people excessively using jargon does not help matters. Jargon is much easier to mishear or misinterpret leading to all kinds of embarrassing situations.

- **When my battery dies in inopportune moments**; This is my fault in part for being ill-prepared – I know that my battery will die roughly three days after changing it (if I don't wear it as much – i.e. weekends when I sleep A LOT – it can last for 4 days) but I don't know exactly when it will die and I'm often caught short. This means I am rendered completely deaf which makes the working environment a minefield, there's only so much lip-reading can help you with after all.

Over time, you learn to adjust and make compromises that help you to hear and communicate better with your colleagues and it is about experimenting to find out what works for you.

Consider the following tips for not only improving your performance in the workplace but also making you feel happier.

- Talk to your boss; I sat down with my manager and discussed how my work environment needed to be changed; in my case, I needed to move desks so that my back was to the wall eliminating background noises and facing the rest of my colleagues. I also needed to adjust the position of my monitors so that I could see my colleagues faces opposite me. Sit down and discuss your own individual needs with your manager.

- If you work with a large team it would be worthwhile speaking to them to highlight how they can communicate effectively with you, let them know whether you read lips so that they can sit in a place where you can clearly see their face etc.

- If you take part in large meetings where PowerPoint presentations are used, ask for a printout beforehand so you can familiarise yourself with the topics being discussed. Likewise, it might be useful to obtain the minutes of the previous meeting so you can make sure there is nothing you have missed. Not only would this show forward thinking on your behalf but it would also alleviate your concerns about missing any vital information.

- Use email as your primary method of communication. Many people with hearing loss find the telephone difficult in normal circumstances but in a loud environment it is near on impossible to understand someone on the telephone. Use email as your first form of communication, if the client/customer/colleague requests telephone communication, refer the matter to someone else.

- Contact Access To Work; This is a government scheme designed to help the disabled get the equipment they need in the workplace. It can be a long process but if you need specialised equipment it is worth pursuing. An assessor will come to your workplace to talk to you about your specific needs and assess your workspace before submitting a report based on their findings. A copy will be sent directly to your employer stating what equipment you need, where to buy it and how much it costs. It is worth remembering that your employer has a legal duty to ensure you have the equipment you need to carry out your job. There are all sorts of equipment that they can suggest that will help you, from text relay telephones to microphones for meetings.

Find out more about the Access to Work scheme here https://www.gov.uk/access-to-work/overview

- If you suffer with tinnitus on a daily basis you might find wearing in-ear headphones in one ear with low music on helpful, music is widely believed to be a factor in reducing the effects of tinnitus. For those with a profound hearing loss this wouldn't be an option but perhaps a radio on with low music might yield the same results, it is just something to keep your brain from focusing on the tinnitus.

- Consider altering your working hours. I found getting public transport during the AM and PM rush hours extremely scary and exhausting and after discussions with my manager, he kindly agreed to alter my working hours so that I would not have to travel when it was extremely busy. This made my life much easier.

- Above all, talk to someone if you are struggling. It is in your employers benefit for you to be happy and confident in your working environment.

In this day and age with so many technological advances, there is no reason why you cannot be a part of the workplace. Just perhaps that telesales job might be a step too far...

Chapter Eight
Travel

Travelling is always exciting, especially when it is to far flung places but when you have hearing loss it can feel daunting and there is plenty of potential for things to go terribly wrong.

Whether travelling by car, bus, train or plane there are plenty of obstacles for the hearing impaired to navigate from missing tannoy announcements to mishearing instructions all of which leave you feeling embarrassed and at times useless.

I have travelled to a fair few places in my 29 years of life and the first year travelling after my SSHL diagnosis was by far the scariest. I constantly feared something going wrong and relied heavily on my partner to help in situations I felt uncomfortable in.

I have now got to a point where I am comfortable travelling, by any means of transport, alone or accompanied and I want to share my top tips with you.

My top tips for travelling with hearing loss and Cochlear Implants;

Before travel;

- **Ask;** If you are at all unsure about anything, ask your audiologists advice.

- **Prepare, prepare and prepare some more;** Make sure you pack spares of just about everything you need for your hearing equipment, you may never need it but it'll ease your mind that they are there in case of emergencies.

- **Research;** This is particularly important if you are travelling alone. Research your routes carefully and print out confirmations of itineraries, hotel stays, transport tickets etc. This will make things easier communication wise for you too.

- **Invest in a phrase book;** If you are travelling abroad, consider buying yourself a basic phrase book so you can at least point to a phrase in a book if you are having issues communicating.

- **Emergency contacts;** As well as making sure your friends and family back home have your itineraries, consider also making sure you have information on the nearest audiology clinic to your destination and a brief synopsis of your medical history in case your equipment breaks or you have an emergency.

  For those who wear a Cochlear implant, look up the nearest implant centre and note down all your current details such as implant model, device make and UK hospital details. It would also be a good idea to obtain a copy of your current "map" from your audiologist.

- **Travel Insurance;** This should be a pre-requisite for anyone travelling but if you are taking specialist equipment with you, make sure this is covered on your insurance.

- **Holiday Loaner Scheme;** If you wear a Cochlear Implant, consider using your manufacturers holiday loaner scheme where you can loan a spare processor mapped to your requirements for a nominal fee.

- **Medical card;** If you have one, bring your medical card stating you have a hearing loss with you, if you do not have one, consider purchasing one through Hearing Link UK. If you have a CI, you should have a patient identification card that explains your implant in several languages, alternatively, google translate some key phrases about the implant in case it is needed.

At the airport / Other ports;

- **Exit Seats;** At checking in (airport) ensure that the staff do not give you a seat by the exit windows, as tempting as it is to have more space, airplane guidance stipulate that those with a hearing loss should not sit in exit seats in case they are given instructions they cannot hear to operate the doors.

- **Body Scan;** If you wear a CI opt for a full body pat down by an officer or go through the body scanner which does not interfere with your implant. Make sure you explain your reasons to the airport staff and show your card if necessary.

- **X-Ray;** If you do for some reason need to go through the X-ray machines, turn off your processor and put it through the scanning machine along with your hand luggage. Make sure you let the staff know you may set the machines off because of your implant.

- **Hand Luggage;** Carry your CI user guide and travel repair kit with you in your hand luggage.

During Travel;

- **Tell Staff;** Make sure a member of staff knows you have a hearing loss, whether air crew, train conductor or coach driver, this way they can inform you of any announcements made separately.

- **Switch Off;** It is recommended that CI users switch off their processors during take off and landing, similar to other electronic devices, but it is not entirely necessary and is a personal choice.

On Holiday;

- **Beach;** If you are in exotic climes (lucky you!) and you have a Cochlear Implant/hearing aid or other equipment, make sure you bring a dry box or waterproof bag with you to avoid moisture getting to the device.

- **Repair Kit;** Make sure you pack your CI/hearing aid repair kit for basic maintenance tools.

Remember, your hearing loss will not affect your ability to travel, you just need to be a bit more prepared than the average traveller. Don't let it affect your enjoyment of your well-earned break!

Chapter Nine
Assistive Equipment

As well as personal, emotional support through charities and other organisations, there is also a wealth of practical support available to you through assistive devices. I haven't had much experience with them aside from hearing aids and the bellman paging system but I wanted to share with you *some* of the excellent devices out there that can make your life easier.

Hearing Aids;

This may sound obvious to some of you but there are many people out there with mild hearing loss who are unaware that hearing aids could help them. They are not just for the more severely deafened, in fact, they could even help those of you with tinnitus! I personally think a lot of people dismiss the idea of hearing aids because they associate them with the older generation.

There are many different types of hearing aids and they have evolved considerably since I had my first analogue ones fitted 27 years ago. When I was little, hearing aids were clunky, weighed quite heavy and were easily noticeable but now they are digital with the thinnest of tubes and are lightweight and discreet. You can even get hearing aids that sit just inside your ear so no need for tubes or behind the ear processors.

It is common sense that the earlier you get a hearing aid following any kind of hearing loss, the more benefit you will receive from them. They are devised of three parts; a microphone, amplifier and speaker. It receives sound from the microphone which converts the sound waves to electrical signals and sends them to the amplifier which then increases the power of the signals and sends them to the ear through the speaker. Basically, it will amplify sounds to a level that you can hear sufficiently.

This means that for those with a severe to profound hearing loss, a hearing aid will not be of benefit to you as it can only amplify sounds already heard.

Hearing aids are available on the NHS free of charge (UK readers), however, some types of hearing aids such as the In-the-ear (ITE), In-the-canal (ITC) and Completely-in-the-canal (CIC) aids are not. However, some time ago it was reported that some NHS audiology departments across the UK were reducing their services and only offering patients one hearing aid instead of two.

You can also buy hearing aids privately, with many high-street companies such as Boots offering audiology services and a wide variety of all types of hearing aids ranging from £345 through to £2,195 per hearing aid. It is important to make sure you know what severity of hearing loss you have and research your options thoroughly to make sure you aren't pushed into purchasing a more expensive aid that you do not necessarily need.

Hearing Loop (or audio induction loop)

Have you ever wondered what the 'T' setting on your hearing aid/implant is for?

If you already have a hearing aid or cochlear implant and need a device to help you pick up speech in crowded rooms, then this could be the device for you.

The hearing loop provides a magnetic, wireless signal that is picked up by your hearing aid when the 'T' (Telecoil) setting is activated. It consists of a microphone, an amplifier and a loop cable. The microphone picks up speech and the amplifier processes this signal and sends it to the loop which is a cable that is placed around the boundary of the specified area and acts as an antenna that radiates magnetic signal to the hearing aid.

The loop is useful in cutting out background noises and making it feel as if the person speaking is standing right next to you. It is apparently readily available in most public spaces; however, many people find that staff are not aware of how to operate the system and often they are left turned off.

Bellman Paging System (Bellman Visit 868 paging system)

I have mentioned my Bellman Paging System several times and I highly recommend it for around the house, even if you do not use it, it gives you peace of mind knowing it is there.

The system is designed to alert you to several different alarms i.e. smoke alarm, telephone, baby monitor, alarm clock and doorbell. You are even able to choose how you want to utilise the receiver, whether you clip it to a piece of clothing, keep it in a cradle on your desktop or wear it around your wrist. In all situations, the receiver will vibrate alerting you to an alarm, the appropriate symbol will also light up to tell you exactly what the noise is.

You can also choose to have a vibrating pad which will alert you to any of the alarms whilst you are asleep. This is especially useful for those who have to take off their hearing aids or cochlear implants at night. The vibrate is powerful and will continue to vibrate until you turn off the system on the receiver.

The device is wireless and easy to set up, although your adult social services department or the company you order it from should be able to help with installation if needed.

Flashing doorbells

There are numerous flashing or vibrating doorbells available through Action on Hearing Loss or Connevans, some of these simply plug into sockets while others are battery operated and can be moved anywhere within the home. They work by emitting a loud ringer and flashing light to alert you to the doorbell.

The only downside to some of these is that there is often a slight time delay.

Textphones or Amplified phones

For the severely deafened, Text phones can be a life saver. These are phones that have a small screen and keyboard attached on which a message can be typed to be received by another text phone. Depending on the model you choose, you can choose whether to type or speak you part of the conversation and receive text back that you can read.

These are widely available through Action on Hearing Loss, Connevans and even some high-street suppliers.

There is also an app for the smart phone/computer or tablet user; the NGT Lite app.

It works by the text user texting their message to the relay assistant who then speaks the words to the phone user, the phone user speaks their reply and the relay assistant types their answer to the text user.

Personal Amplifiers

Personal amplifiers can be body worn or hand held and can help you to hear what is being said in a one to one or small group environments. For those with a mild hearing loss and who do not wear hearing aids, there are earphones and headphones available. For those with hearing aids a neck loop is provided to listen through the aids.

You just place the amplifier on the table (or wherever you are) in front of the personal speaking and your earphones/headphones or neck loop will pick up the speech clearly, with no interference. You can also use personal amplifiers to listen to the TV in settings where simply turning up the volume is not possible.

Whatever your needs, there are many devices out there that can help you to hear more clearly. Always obtain advice from an audiologist on what particular devices might be suitable for you as each device offers different solutions.

Chapter Ten

Cochlear Implants

Cochlear Implants are relatively new to the world with the first Cochlear Implant patient receiving a device in 1978, that was only 39 years ago!

Given their short medical history, there is a lot of confusion around CI's and their benefits, I certainly didn't know anything about the devices when it was first mentioned to me.

For those who are not aware, a Cochlear Implant comprises of two separate parts; the internal part and the external part. The internal part consists of a receiver magnet and electrodes, this is inserted behind your ear into your skull during an operation, the electrodes are then inserted into your cochlea.

The external device looks similar to a hearing aid except that there is a transmitter magnet attached by a short coil which connects to the receiver magnet when switched on. The transmitter will receive sounds externally and then send electronic signals through the receiver and down to the electrodes which will simulate the natural cochlea hairs and send vibrations to your brain which will interpret these signals into sounds. Amazing, right?

There are three main manufacturers of Cochlear Implants that the NHS offer, these being Med-El, Advanced Bionics and Cochlear. Whilst all three of these manufacturers essentially produce the same product, some devices differ in software and aesthetics. As

Cochlear Implant results are subjective, there is little information in the public domain regarding real results and what benefit they provide for individuals and so choosing a device can be a difficult process.

Before you can even consider choosing a device, there will be a process you will need to go through to obtain an implant which can be long, tedious and frustrating at times. Here in the UK, the NICE guidelines set criteria for eligibility and is often considered too rigid. The NICE criteria states that to be eligible for an implant you must have a hearing loss that is severe to profound and you must have tried hearing aids for at least 3 months with no benefit gained.

Bilateral implants are accepted for children and for adults who have another form of disability such as blindness, where they would rely on sound for spatial awareness. But for those who do not fit into this category, currently only one implant is allowed for adults.

Severe to profound hearing loss is defined as hearing sounds that are louder than 90 dB HL at frequencies of 2 and 4kHZ without hearing aids[5]. The following diagram shows how this could look on an audiogram.

[5] https://www.nice.org.uk/guidance/TA166/chapter/1-guidance

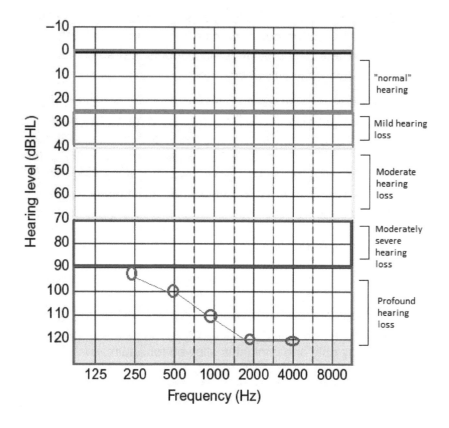

It is stated that adequate benefit from hearing aids is defined as a score of 50% or more on an open set speech perception test, or for children, speech, language and listening skills appropriate for their age.

The problem with this is that these tests are conducted in a soundproofed and eerily silent room. You have been prepared by the audiologist to listen for sounds and know when they are going to happen; none of this is representative of real life where background noise is constant and varying.

What also isn't fully clarified in the NICE criteria is that if one of your ears has some benefit from hearing aids, or is over the required decibel range – even slightly, you are not eligible for an implant, regardless of whether this would be the implanted ear or not.

The NICE criteria doesn't give any consideration for the environmental factors – the everyday noises that are part and parcel of life; traffic, background music and conversations. There are no circumstances in life where everything is deathly silent (apart from your school exams perhaps – shudder!), where you can fully focus on one sound so why does the criteria for determining whether you can be given the gift of hearing again rely so heavily on these results?

During the process of obtaining the implant you can expect a myriad of hearing tests and scans to try to determine not only the cause of your profound hearing loss but also whether any medical conditions require you to have a particular device. You will undertake assessments that not only test your hearing ability but also your lip-reading ability and your speech; these are all aspects that will help the implant team to determine whether you are suitable

Once you are deemed suitable, the hard work begins.

First you will need to choose your device, the UK currently offer three main manufacturers; Advanced Bionics, Med-El and Cochlear. I cannot stress enough how important it is to do your own research independent of your specialists advice, not only because you will gain a better understanding of how the device works but it will help you to feel in control of the situation. This is something that will impact on you for the rest of your life and only you will know what you want from the implant. Do bear in mind though that ultimately, they all serve the same purpose; to restore a sense of hearing to the patient.

My top tips for choosing a device;

- Have a look at all of the manufacturers websites and draw up a list of attributes of their devices. Remember to not rely on this information too much, they are of course, going to sing their own praises and you need unbiased information at this stage.

- Work out what is the most important aspect of hearing for you; ie. Music/conversational speech etc.

- Look at the recall rates. There are sometimes issues with devices that cause a manufacturer to halt production or recall devices due to safety concerns, this is something that could hinder your rehabilitation and is important to bear in mind.

- Look at the options for upgrading in the future. Will the implant you have chosen be compatible with future upgrades?

- Dig around the internet to find out past patient's speech perception scores with the varying implants on offer. Obviously, as pointed out before, this is subjective but it might help you to get an idea of what to expect.

- Look into the accessories they offer – if you are a keen swimmer, you might like to look at their waterproof options etc.

Do remember, whatever device you choose, your audiologist is going to have the same skill and knowledge about the device, accessories and rehabilitation – they are not affiliated with any one manufacturer!

You may be invited to your hospital to view the implants on offer which is extremely helpful, your audiologist will explain a little about each device and the accessories on offer and you will get to see how similar they are in look. The only difference really is the colour options available to you. You may, depending on the hospital, also have a Cochlear Implantee there to talk you through their own personal experiences. If you do, utilise that – ask them everything you want to know, that's what they are there for!

I also urge you to keep your expectations in check. You will have a meeting with your speech therapist and audiologist about expectations from your implant and they do encourage you to keep them realistic. Do not expect immediate clarity and sound when you are first switched on!

The surgery

Scary word isn't it, surgery?

In fact, it really isn't. Of course, there are risks, as with any surgery, but these are relatively rare; the main concern is the increased risk of contracting meningitis so you are required to have an up to date inoculation before your operation but besides this, it is pretty routine.

Now my experience may be different to others, as all hospitals are different and procedures vary UK wide but I will give you a brief outline of what to expect before, during and post-surgery.

- A lot of waiting; I was admitted to hospital at 7.30am and my surgery didn't take place until 10.30ish!

- A lot of questions; the ward sister will ask you about your health, previous surgery, allergies as well as general questions so be prepared!

- A lot of forms; obviously as with all surgeries, you will need to sign consent forms, and there are lots of them.

- A loss of dignity; who designed these hospital gowns?

- To not be able to hear; when I was prepped for surgery and my glasses and hearing aids were taken off me, the consultant started asking me questions, I couldn't hear or see him so was a little distressed.

- A bit of dribbling; when I lost consciousness from the anaesthetic, I dribbled quite a bit, as if I wasn't embarrassed enough.

- A 2-4-hour surgery (this may be longer depending on medical needs) not that you will know.

- To wake up, but not be awake; once I had the surgery and was wheeled back to my little room, I woke up but was not all there. I was apparently having extremely odd conversations which I do not remember at all.

- A bit of pain. Again, this will be subjective as everyone has different pain thresholds but there is to be expected, a bit of discomfort.

- To be discharged the same day; in some circumstances, there may be cause for an overnight stay but generally it is a day surgery.

- To be really aware of the implant; I noticed on my way home that every time the car went over a bump, I could feel something inside my head. It was very bizarre.

- To not be able to wash your hair for two weeks; Gross, right? As the wound heals, you need to keep it dry and that means no washing of hair until you get the all clear from the hospital.

- To not be able to hear in implanted ear; you will not be allowed to wear hearing aids in that ear so you have a period of no hearing at all.

- A feeling of emptiness in the implanted ear; I remember feeling as if something large had been taken out of my ear and it felt very empty.

- A scar, cool!

So, you see, surgery doesn't need to be scary!

The Switch on

You've had the surgery, had two weeks of gross hair and now you're ready to be switched on. This is the exciting but underwhelming part!

The switch on day itself can be underwhelming for patients as they expect to be able to hear straight away and with perfect clarity; this isn't the case, for anyone.

- You may find that all you can hear is beeps or whistles; this is perfectly fine.

- You may find that you can hear sounds but not distinguish words; this is perfectly fine.

- You may find that voices are robotic sounding; this is perfectly fine.

- You may find that voices are high pitched and tinny; this is perfectly fine.

- You may find that things sound different to how you remembered them, for me keyboards sounded very strange.

Everyone's brain reacts in a different way and for those who have been without natural hearing for a longer period of time, it may take time before you can get any benefit from the implant. It is important not to give up or feel upset.

Some implantee's do not receive full benefit from their implants until a year or so down the line as their brain is constantly adapting and recognising new sounds that it hasn't heard before – do not panic.

The activation day is a long day and you *will* feel tired. Your brain is working overtime to adjust, adapt and recognise these new sounds and you will be concentrating hard so after a few hours you will feel like you have been hit by a bus and want to crawl under the covers. This is a normal reaction and you *should* rest.

A good way to approach this and avoid becoming overtired is to wear your implant for a set number of hours, increasing daily so that eventually you are wearing it full time without feeling exhausted.

If you would like more information on Cochlear Implants, there are several useful websites out there with a wealth of information, below are a few I have utilised myself;

- https://earfoundation.org.uk/hearing-technologies/cochlear-implants/cochlear-implant-centres-in-the-uk - A full list of the Cochlear Implant centres/hospitals across the UK.
- http://www.oticonmedical.com/~asset/cache.ashx?id=43834&type=14&format=web – Step by step PDF guide to Cochlear Implantation.
- https://auditoryneuroscience.com/prosthetics/noise_vocoded_speech - Link to a audio file explaining how implants sound to users.
- http://ais.southampton.ac.uk/cochlear-implants/what-does-a-cochlear-implant-sound-like/ - Simulation programme if sounds that may help you to discover what an implant can sound like.

Chapter Eleven

Rehabilitation

Speech and language therapy is an important aspect of your rehabilitation. As well as the regular appointments you will have with your therapist at the hospital, it is vital you continue to work on this in your own time daily. The more you work on retraining your brain, the more benefit you are likely to gain from the implant.

Around your home

Your home harbours a wealth of resources and tools that you can utilise for your rehabilitation; simple things like running the taps, boiling the kettle and opening and closing doors are all sounds that you have to get used to again, or possibly even for the first time. It is important that you take the time to properly listen and try to categorise the sounds so that next time you hear them you can immediately identify the noise.

My Top tips for rehabilitation around your home:

- Ring the doorbell – this is a noise that is likely to be heard on a daily basis.

- Call your home phone – again, it is likely that your phone will ring at least once a day (pesky telemarketers).

- Run the taps.

- Boil the kettle.

- Record these sounds in a journal; write down how it sounded to you, what distinguishing factors there were (i.e. was the sound tinny/loud/etc) so that you can look back on this and can easily identify the noise.

Television

The TV is another extremely useful tool and is one that I utilised most during my own rehabilitation. I watched TV shows that I had never watched before, particularly ones I knew accents would be prominent, such as Geordie Shore. I found this useful to me (and very amusing) as accents can be difficult to understand at the best of times, let alone distinguishing between male and female accents.

My top tips for TV rehabilitation are as follows;

- Choose a TV programme where the accent is different to your own or quite heavy.

- Watch the first episode with the subtitles on so you can easily follow along.

- For the second episode take the subtitles off and see how much you can follow without support; try not to concentrate on lip-reading too much either.

- If you are feeling really confident, why don't you try closing your eyes and listening, try and figure out if you can work out not only what they are saying but if it was a male or female voice.

- In addition to this, have the TV on low in the background regularly as this will help you to normalise sounds and create background noises that are part and parcel of everyday life.

Audio Books

Another important tool that can be utilised on the go are Audio Books, this is useful for everyday brain training as you can download the book onto your phone and take it with you wherever you go.

In fact, Audible recently published an article[6] all about the positive effect audio books can have on cochlear implant rehabilitation and I was interviewed by a New York journalist about how I utilised audio books for my own development.

My top tips for utilising Audio Books are;

- For your first attempts, download a book you are already familiar with and one that you have a hard copy of.

- Follow the story with your hard copy so you can familiarise yourself with the voice, inflictions and pace.

- Once you feel confident, dismiss the hard copy and listen along. Because you are already familiar with the content, your brain should (in theory) bridge the gaps if you miss some words.

- Once you have familiarised yourself with books you already know, purchase/download books you have never ready before.

---

[6] http://www.audiblerange.com/categories/the-listening-life/a-new-chapter-for-the-hearing-impaired/

- Also try to choose books that may have a different reader to your usual choices, i.e. if you usually read "chick lit" with female narrators, go for a genre where it is likely a male will be narrating.

Remember; the voices used in audio books generally are quite deadpan and monotonous and this will sound different to "normal" voices.

Online / Apps;

There are numerous apps and websites out there that can help you on your hearing journey, some are more detailed and advanced than others; I have detailed some of the ones I found useful below;

www.angelsound.tigerspeech.com

Billed as an "interactive listening rehabilitation and functional hearing test programme", this programme is an excellent starting point for the new implant users. There are several different modules to choose from; Basic, Noise, Telephone, Melodic, Openset, Music, Auditory, Assessment and Scene based.

The basic module will give you options of pure tone discrimination, environmental sounds, male/female identification, vowel recognition, consonant recognition, word discrimination, everyday sentences and music appreciation.

For the beginner, I would suggest starting with the environmental sounds, word discrimination and everyday sentences as these are likely to be sounds/words/phrases you will hear regularly.

Each module will give you a brief introduction and a chance to preview sounds before beginning your training, I recommend previewing the sounds beforehand. You will be given a choice of levels from 1-4, with 1 being the easiest and 4 the hardest. At level 4 background noises will be present whilst sentences/words are spoken and will be more comparable to everyday situations.

Each module has a test, the tests consist of an American voice speaking a word/phrase or whole sentence and you will then be presented with a multiple-choice question based on what was said. Sometimes you are presented with pictures representing the sound or noises heard.

I personally found the voice to be quite monotonous and quiet - so be alert!

A word of warning: this programme will need to be downloaded from your computer/laptop and is not compatible with Mac computers or iPads. There is however, a CD version available upon request.

www.ABsoundsuccess.com

You can obtain a month free trial from your audiologist and I recommend doing so.

This programme gives you the opportunity to practice listening to people having a conversation; you are given a variety of topics to choose from and the gender of the speaker. Once selected, a video will play showing two people having a conversation on the topic you have chosen.

Following the video, you will be faced with a few questions on what was discussed. It tests both your memory and your listening skills.

What I found annoying about this particular programme is that the two speakers were clearly over enunciating and speaking particularly slowly for the video, I felt it was too contrived, however, others may find it useful in the early stages of rehabilitation.

http://www.cochlear.com/wps/wcm/connect/uk/home/support/rehabilitation-resources/hope-words

I have also recently discovered that Cochlear have created an auditory rehabilitation app for iPads and iPhones called HOPE words. This is aimed at improving the listening and spoken language skills of children with hearing loss. To find out more, have a look at the above link.

www.medel.com/us/soundscape/

Med-El have developed several online games which are designed to help you test your listening skills. There are different games designed for different age groups. For adults, they have developed Sentence Matrix and Sentence Matrix 2. Both of these tools are designed for practising speech recognition whilst reading sentences.

You can choose to hear a female or male voice and can adjust the sound easily to fit your personal requirements. You are also required to choose the number of sentences tested from 10, 20 or 30 and can also choose the type of background noise you would like, such as, music. This is a good tool for simulating real life experiences and is highly recommended.

Telephone

It is imperative to bear in mind that not all Cochlear Implantees can hear on the telephone, or hear well but it is an important aspect of your brain training, although it can be a very frustrating one.

I personally find mobile phones easier than analogue phones because it is a clearer connection; you may wish to begin on a mobile and advance up to an analogue. I would advise that you still sign up to the 999-text relay service in any event, as discussed earlier, just in case.

My Top Tips for using the telephone;

- If you have access to one, use a mobile phone before an analogue phone.

- For your first attempt, call the speaking clock or your local cinema for film times – these are automated and will help you gauge how much you can hear through the phone.

- Ask a family member or friend to ring you and talk about a pre-determined subject. This will mean that if you cannot quite hear what they are saying or miss a word, you can bridge the gaps a bit as you know the topic being discussed. Although it seems a little pointless, it will help you build up your confidence.

- Ask your family member or friend to draw a picture and then describe said picture over the phone to you whilst you draw it. Then compare the two pictures and see if you heard their instructions correctly – a fun little task!

- If you find yourself on the phone to someone you have never spoken to before, preface your conversation by telling them you have a hearing loss and asking them to speak clearly – people generally are willing to oblige if you are upfront with them.

Face to Face

A novel concept in these modern times, but face to face speech and listening exercises are the best rehabilitation tools you can utilise. It would be beneficial to you to be able to practise these exercises with a mix of male and female family members/friends but this isn't always possible.

For most people the tricky aspect of rehabilitation are the words that sound similar like;

Eye/pie/my

He/she/me

Fat/mat/pat

Pour/more/four

So why not practise these singular words with Word Bingo. Ask your friend/family member to identify words you struggle with and write these down. Categorise them into similar sounding groups and create bingo cards like shown below;

Eye	He	Fat	Pour
Pie	She	Mat	More
My	Me	Pat	Four

Each of you will have a bingo card in front of you and your nominated person will call out the words (whilst covering their mouth – this part is important!) and you cross off the words as they are called out.

This exercise will not only help you to learn sounds that are difficult for you but will do it in a way that is fun and light hearted.

Although a lot of these exercises can be carried out in your home, don't forget that there is a wealth of opportunity for rehabilitation in the outside world! You will find that by being outside you are learning new things all the time, the sound of traffic, birds tweeting, children chattering away etc and it is all being processed by your brain. The more you can get outside and go to new places, the more you are training your brain to recognise common sounds without much effort on your part!

The most important piece of advice I can give to someone considering an implant or going through the process is not to give up. It takes perseverance, determination and time and you are the only person who can change your life for the best – a year or two of hard work is small fry for a lifetime of being able to hear your loved ones talking to you, being involved in your friends and families lives and feeling in control of your own future.

Chapter Twelve

My Journey Continues

At the time of writing this book, it has been two years since I underwent surgery for my cochlear implant and close to two years since the dreaded activation day. Back then I couldn't have imagined how much it would have turned my life around.

I would never have thought that a magnet in my skull would give me my life back.

I had hoped of course, that I would be able to get some semblance of my normal life back and gain a bit more confidence in tackling the big bad world by myself, but it has given me so much more than that.

I feel more confident, not only in day to day activities, but also in myself. The journey I have taken has proved that I am strong and capable and now that I have my CI, there is no stopping me. My relationships with friends, family and colleagues have improved drastically because I am now able to communicate with them effectively and join in with social events, something I have thoroughly enjoyed!

I have travelled half way around the world since my implant, got married, started up a blog and now, written a book. All these things, whilst still possible with my hearing loss, have been even more exciting and enjoyable because I have felt a part of it all, felt *visible* and included.

Opportunities, socially and professionally, are now there for me to grab hold with both hands. Nothing is impossible anymore.

My whole journey these past few years has taught me to never take anything for granted because it can be taken from you suddenly, and without reason. It has made me more grateful for all the positives I have in my life and incredibly appreciative of all the support I have had from my family, friends, colleagues, Charities and strangers.

Whilst it is generally true that 'deafness separates us from people'[7], the support and love I received proves that this isn't always the case.

---

[7] https://en.wikiquote.org/wiki/Helen_Keller

End Note

I hope that this book has helped you in some way, whether it is just by realising you are not alone in your struggles or whether it's through the helpful tips and hints throughout.

Knowing you are not alone is key, so many of us with hearing loss struggle with the feelings of isolation and loneliness but help is out there. I have outlined just *some* of the charities/organisations and people that can help you but there are so many more.

If you are feeling frustrated with what little you feel you can do, try to utilise some of the helpful advice I have provided, you will be surprised by how something so simple can make such a difference. It's about taking control.

I'm not going to lie and say dealing with any form of hearing loss is an easy transition because it isn't, not in any way, shape or form but by adapting your lifestyle and adopting some of the methods I have spoken about in this book, you can start to feel more confident and independent.

If your family and friends are struggling to identify with what you are going through or how to help you, show them this book and hopefully they will begin to get a clearer idea of your day to day struggles and how it impacts on your confidence, friendships and general life.

Thank you again to everyone who has supported me on my hearing loss journey and has helped to bring this book to life – you support is so valued.

And of course, all of this wouldn't have been possible without the support, guidance and expertise of my ENT consultant Dr Hariri, my surgeon Mr Khalil and all of the audiology and speech therapy team at Royal National Ear

Nose Throat Hospital – my heartfelt thanks go to all of you for making this my reality.

Glossary

ENT – Ear Nose Throat

SSHL – Sudden Sensorineural Hearing Loss

CI – Cochlear Implant

AB – Advanced Bionics

ITE – In the ear

BTE – behind the ear

ITC- In the canal

CIC – Completely in canal

NGT – Next Generation Text

AoHL – Action on Hearing Loss

HL – Hearing Link

dBHL – Decibel

HZ - Frequency

Useful Links

Hearing Link: www.hearinglink.org

Action On Hearing Loss: www.actiononhearingloss.org.uk

Restored Hearing: www.restoredhearing.com

NHS Online: www.nhs.uk

Access To Work: www.gov.uk/access-to-work

The Invisible Disability And Me:
www.theinvisibledisabilityandme.co.uk

Connevans: www.connevans.co.uk

Deaf Equipment Online: www.deafequipment.co.uk

British Cochlear Implant Group: www.bcig.org.uk

Emergency Services Text Relay: www.emergencysms.org.uk

Audible: www.audible.co.uk

Med-El : www.medel.com

Cochlear: www.cochlear.com

Advanced Bionics: www.advancedbionics.com

UK based Cochlear Implant Centres:
http://www.earfoundation.org.uk/hearing-technologies/cochlear-implants/cochlear-implant-centres-in-the-uk

USA advice for selecting a Cochlear Implant Surgeon:
http://thehearingblog.com/archives/4216

L - #0258 - 050623 - C0 - 210/148/5 - PB - DID3598071